D0374890

The Little Book of
WEDDING ETIQUETTE

by HOLLY LEFEVRE

Running Press
PHILADELPHIA · LONDON

© 2013 by Running Press
Illustrations © 2013 by Trina Dalziel
Published by Running Press,
A Member of the Perseus Books Group

Books published by Running Press are available at
special discounts for bulk purchases in the United States
by corporations, institutions, and other organizations. For more
information, please contact the Special Markets Department at the
Perseus Books Group, 2300 Chestnut Street, Suite 200, Philadelphia,
PA 19103, or call (800) 810-4145, ext. 5000, or e-mail
special.markets@perseusbooks.com.

ISBN 978-0-7624-5043-5
Library of Congress Control Number: 2012955852

E-book ISBN 978-0-7624-5036-7

9   8   7   6   5   4   3   2   1
Digit on the right indicates the number of this printing

Cover and interior design by Amanda Richmond
Edited by Jennifer Leczkowski
Typography: Archer and Lavanderia

Running Press Book Publishers
2300 Chestnut Street
Philadelphia, PA 19103-4371

Visit us on the web!
www.runningpress.com

Contents

Introduction

Weddings are about tradition and pomp and circumstance and celebration . . . and of course, love. If only it was that "easy." Combined with those fun and fanciful aspects of a wedding are emotions, sensitivities, families, and the rules of proper wedding etiquette. There is etiquette that has stood the test of time, and here is etiquette that has evolved and been adapted for modern couples. In the fast-paced ever-changing world we live in, knowing what is proper can help guide you as you plan your wedding or even go about your daily life.

Our world changes on a daily basis, and with that what we as a society consider to be "right" and "wrong" also changes. Weddings and wedding etiquette are keeping up with the times. Ten or fifteen years ago, the rules for wedding parties were changing as more and more couples were having grooms-women and Men of Honor. Now we are contending with cellphones ringing during ceremonies, balancing blended families, and how to show respect to same-sex couples and marriages. As times change, etiquette needs to change to accommodate the modern world.

One thing is very true ... expect the unexpected. Every wedding is unique and when you are dealing with people and emotions, you never know what to expect—but you can be prepared. When faced with uncertainty, a bride can turn to *The Little Book of Wedding Etiquette* as a quick and easy reference for the most common etiquette challenges. Simple, easy-to-read advice for the most common modern dilemmas are in the pages of this little book, so throw it in your purse or bag and you can always be ready with an answer!

As you plan your wedding you will be faced with many decisions and many times you must decide what the right thing to do is. Essentially this is etiquette. The number one rule is to be kind and respectful. Ask yourself: "Is this how I would want to be treated?" "Would this make me feel awkward if I was the guest?" This book will guide you as you plan and prepare for this most magnificent day in your life. So go on, enjoy yourself. Be a gracious bride and a gracious host and enjoy this amazing time in your life.

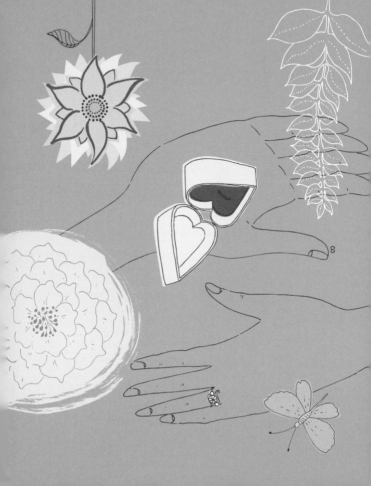

Chapter 1:

The Engagement

A wedding is something many women have been dreaming of since they were little girls. Gorgeous gowns, beautiful flowers, elegant music, and diamonds are synonymous with weddings! Some women have been dreaming about this day for a long time, others only started to think about it once the ring was on their finger. No matter the case, a bride-to-be often doesn't realize the amount of planning that needs to take place before that magical day.

DOES ANYONE STILL ASK PERMISSION?

At one time it was a groom's duty, obligation even, to meet with a bride's parents and ask permission for her hand in marriage. With modern couples living independently and making their own decisions regarding their life, asking permission is a largely ceremonial act that is currently done to accommodate a bride or groom's preference or cultural and religious traditions.

When deciding whether or not to ask permission, a groom (and bride) must take all things into consideration. Some religions and many cultures view a man asking permission for a woman's hand as a necessity and a sign of respect. Additionally, the parents of younger adults (those of legal age but maybe still in college, living at home, etc.) may also expect the courtesy of being asked permission. Still, some brides, no matter how savvy or independent they are in life, find themselves embracing long-standing traditions when it comes to their wedding planning, and may expect their boyfriends to ask permission before proposing.

RING CONSIDERATIONS

A wedding is about love and celebrating a union of two people, but let's be honest, the ring is an integral part of the Western wedding and engagement ritual. Many conversations will begin with "Can I see the ring?" That does not mean the ring needs to be big. It does not mean that your fiancé needs to break the bank—that two-months salary rule no longer applies. It does not mean that you have to have a diamond. And technically, you do not really have to have a ring to call it an engagement (but not many women will go for that!). What a ring does need to symbolize is the fact that time, care, consideration, and love went into the selection and purchase of this special, life-long piece of jewelry.

Traditionally, the man typically shops for and makes the ring decisions by himself, but traditions are being rewritten every day. Many ladies shop right alongside their significant others for the engagement ring. It does take some—or all—of the surprise out of this, but many couples feel it is appropriate and important as it ensures the lady gets just what she wants—a ring that ultimately reflects her personal style (and is one that he can afford).

A diamond engagement ring has become almost expected. The purchase of a diamond is a major investment, and your fiancé (or you) should research the criteria known as The Four C's, as they affect the final value and price of the stone.

The Four C's are:

Clarity: Measures the flaws and imperfections on the diamond.

Cut: Refers to the actual configuration or shape of the stone.

Color: Refers to the stone's color. The most desirable are colorless stones, but in recent times yellow diamonds, pink diamonds, and other variations have become trendy.

Carat: Refers to the size and weight of the stone.

There are ring options beyond a diamond engagement ring. An heirloom ring, passed down from either side of the family, can be a treasured and truly special way to express a couple's love and commitment. If the engagement is a surprise, there is always the chance that an heirloom ring may not be exactly what you had in mind. In such situations, there needs to be discussion with your fiancé and that particular side of the family, explaining the reasons, as well as presenting some alternative ideas, such as accepting the ring but ultimately wearing the ring on the other hand.

Colored gemstones, such as the bride's favorite stone or her birthstone are options as well. With the amazing jewelry designers out there, even bands of precious metals are also options for en engagement ring. Who's to say you cannot celebrate your love and commitment with a birthstone or your favorite gemstone … or no stone at all?

While much attention is paid to the bride's engagement ring, you will also need to consider the wedding bands. The wedding bands are a symbol of the marriage rather than simply the engagement. The rings will be exchanged during the ceremony. Some women do forgo a separate wedding band, but most find a band that complements the style of the engagement ring so that they may wear them together after the wedding. The man's wedding band can be simple or ornate, reflecting his personal style, and the bands do not need to match one another.

On the wedding day the engagement ring should be slipped onto your right hand prior to the ceremony. During the ring exchange your ring finger should be bare and awaiting your wedding band, as the wedding band is worn "closest to your heart." After the ceremony, once that wedding band has been placed upon your finger, slide the engagement ring back on the ring finger.

ANNOUNCEMENTS

Maybe you have waited years, maybe you have waited months, maybe it was a surprise, but now you have a ring on your finger and want everyone to know about your happiness. But before you grab the phone or hit the internet to start spreading the word . . . STOP! Your mom may not appreciate hearing the news from your best friend's babysitter while in line at the grocery store. For some things, there is no substitute. Telling your parents and other important people in your life needs to be taken care of the old-fashioned way.

It is becoming a rare circumstance for today's families to all live in one city or even state. People live all over the country, and even all over the world, so you just need to do your best to make the announcement special and meaningful no matter who lives where, who you are telling, or how many times you need to tell it.

Officially, here is the order in which you spread the news:

- **Children of either party**
  (if there are any)
- **Bride's parents** (if divorced, the parent who raised you should be told first, then the other parent)

- **Groom's parents** (if divorced, the parent who raised you should be told first, then the other parent)

If either the bride or groom have children, telling them the news of the engagement should be the first priority. It is of the utmost importance to make sure the children feel a part of the new family. Correspondence with the ex-spouse or boyfriend/girlfriend (in whichever way best suits your current relationship) is in order when children are involved. If both the bride or groom have an ex-spouse and no children are involved then the decision is clearly based upon the relationship between the exes.

Once all of the immediate and closest family members are told, it is time to announce the good news to the rest of the world! Close friends (although you may have already told your best friend) and other family members should be told next. Once those closest to you have been told, you are free to spread the word! In many cases the news of the engagement will have traveled quickly.

Some couples will be enticed to announce the news on all forms of social media—this is a tricky subject. Before you start tweeting or updating Facebook statuses, really think about the ramifications of it. Will all of your Facebook friends think they are invited? Will a distant cousin who thinks she is closer to you than you think she is be offended that this is how she found out? Ultimately making the decision of whether or not to post such great news on social media is your own and you will have to weigh the pros and cons of doing so. If you do decide to post your news via social media, be sure to wait a few weeks so that you can ensure as many people who need to be told in person have been told that way. A simple change in your relationship status is acceptable and may be the best way to announce the news.

There are other appropriate ways to reach a large audience with your announcement. Publishing an engagement announcement in the newspapers of your hometown, current town, and sometimes college town is one way to share your news. You will need to contact each publication, as each has its own requirements and guidelines. You may also consider sending (printed) engagement announcements, which provide a formality to the news. Information about the engagement, names of the couple, and location of the wedding and hosts of the event should be included. Traditionally, the announcements are issued by the bride's parents. Do not send an announcement to anyone who will not be invited to the wedding.

Once the parents are told, it is traditional that the groom's parents reach out to the bride's parents to extend their congratulations. If possible, the two sets of parents should try to find a time to meet in person. If they live far apart, the particulars of a meeting are a bit trickier. If either the bride's or groom's parents are divorced, then the parent who raised the bride/groom should make the phone call. If the bride or groom has not met the other's parents, steps should be taken right away to make a meeting possible. If that meeting cannot take place right away, a sweet note can help break the ice. Be sure to make this meeting a priority.

THE ENGAGEMENT PARTY

What better way to celebrate your love and this milestone in your life than with an engagement party? The engagement party marks the beginning of the wedding celebrations, so it should be held soon after the engagement is announced, ensuring that it will not interfere with any other wedding parties or events. The bride's parents typically plan and host the engagement party. Sometimes the party is held in the bride's (or possibly groom's) hometown, but if a couple has been living away from their families for awhile, it may make more sense to host the party where the couple currently lives so that their friends may attend.

The groom's family may want to host their own party as well, or if the parents are agreeable to it, a joint engagement party may be the perfect solution. An engagement party is by no means a "must," and not every couple has one, but if someone offers to throw you one, go ahead and enjoy!

Do not assume that an engagement party means you will be showered with fabulous gifts. Many guests will bring an engagement gift, but gifts are not "required" elements of an engagement party. Just in case, consider beginning a gift registry for those who do wish to bring a gift. The stores you register with may provide registry cards, but please do not include those cards in the invitation.

SOCIAL MEDIA AND MORE

It is so tempting to announce your plans and share your joy via social media, but you need to be very careful for so many reasons. You must take others feelings into account. Chances are everyone on Facebook is not invited to your wedding so you have to consider whether they might feel a little left out. Does the whole world need to know what you are doing step by step in the planning? Do you really want to be tweeting, in essence: "Hey, I am on my honeymoon far, far away and I have a house full of money and gifts?" (It is not that hard to find out personal information online.)

On the other hand maintaining a wedding website that keeps guests up-to-date on the activities and arrangements being made for the wedding is a helpful tool. It can help the guests navigate the information and make preparations. A wedding blog may do the same thing, but don't get carried away and post every single detail ... there needs to be magic on the wedding day!

Chapter 2

The Wedding Plan

You can plan a wedding on your own. Your mom can help. Your best friend can help. It is your wedding, you can plan it (almost) however you want. But, wouldn't it be nice to have some help? Surrounding yourself with reliable professionals and trustworthy friends as members of the wedding party is essential in keeping calm and can make all the difference in how much you enjoy the day.

CHOOSING THE WEDDING PARTY

Being a part of the wedding party is a big honor. The wedding party should be made up of your closest friends and family. As a member of the wedding party, there are parties to plan and events to attend, but it also comes with responsibilities that need to be taken seriously.

Being a member of the wedding party is a big financial consideration. When someone accepts your invitation, they are agreeing to put forth a large amount of cash and many, many hours of their valuable time. The hosts of the wedding should offer to pay for or assist in finding housing for the attendants when they travel to town for the wedding. If they choose other arrangements, then they are responsible for the fees. Some brides, if they can find it in their budgets, do offer to pay for the attendant's attire, but it is not necessary or expected.

The following is a list of typical financial responsibilities for the wedding party.

- Their attire (dresses or tuxedos) and accessories (shoes, jewelry)
- A gift for the bridal shower(s)
- Contribution to the finances for the bridal shower
- Contribution to the finances for the bachelorette party
- Travel expenses
- A wedding gift

Some men and women receive an "extra honor" when they are asked to be the Maid/Matron of Honor or Best Man. Honor attendants are selected because they hold extra special meaning in your life: your confidant, best friend, or brother/sister, for example. They are your greatest ally during the process, so selecting someone who is responsible, efficient, and willing to help is of the utmost importance. Many brides have a hard time selecting between a sister and a best friend, and there is no reason you cannot have two honor attendants. Just be sure the two like each other and can work together.

There is no rule as to how many or how few attendants you should have, although typically more formal weddings have more attendants. There is no rule saying that a bride cannot have a male attendant or vice versa. And, there is also no rule saying that you must have the same number of attendants on each side. The rules for what is proper, as far as bridal parties go, have loosened up a lot.

It is rather simple to accommodate the new rules of wedding parties.

Here are some easy tips for men serving on the bride's side:

- He can be included in all the normal bridal activities, although he may choose to skip the more girlie aspects of planning and preparation like the bridal shower, bachelorette party, or helping you get dressed.

- He can assist and accompany you in any way you and he feel comfortable.

- On the wedding day, he should wear attire similar to the groomsmen's attire.

- You can distinguish him with a slightly different boutonniere or tie.

Tips for ladies serving as the groom's attendant:

- She may want to skip out on the bachelor party, but other than that can be there to help the groom in whatever way is most comfortable.
- She can wear the same dress as the bridesmaids or a black dress to blend with the men and distinguish herself as a member on his side of the wedding party.
- She can carry a bouquet or even wear a small corsage.
- On the wedding day, she can participate in all groomsmen activities and duties, but should not escort female guests to their seats.
- In addition to the groomsmen, ushers may be needed. Expect to need one

usher for every fifty guests. Ushers are important to the flow of the wedding, as they facilitate seating, assist the guests, and help with other ceremonial duties. They can also remind the guests to turn their cellphones off or set to vibrate. Ushers do not necessarily have to be official groomsmen, but groomsmen can be ushers.

PROFESSIONALLY PLANNED OR DIY?

A wedding planner can work with you in whatever capacity you desire, from "holding your hand" through the process to orchestrating the wedding day to offering simple advice on vendors and attire. When you meet with prospective planners, just ask how they work and only hire one with whom you feel truly comfortable. Don't let the "fear factor" of price steer you away from looking for a planner, there are wedding planners available for all budgets! Even the most organized, particular, stylish bride cannot do it all. Just take some time to think of the advantages a planner can afford you. Following is a simple list of what a planner can do:

- Provide location recommendations.
- Provide professional vendor referrals.
- Offer suggestions and advice on all wedding-related matters.
- Assist with design and styling.
- Act as a liaison between vendors.
- Develop itineraries, confirm reservations and details, and manage logistics.
- Most importantly, oversee all of the

carefully laid plans leading up to and on the wedding day, so that you and your family can enjoy this magical moment.

Wedding planners can be hired at any point in the planning, and knock a hundred or so hours off your research time. The sooner you hire one, the sooner you get to benefit from their years of experience and their amazing contacts. If you cannot afford a wedding planner to help with it all, consider a planner to help you finalize the details and manage the wedding day. The last thing any bride or groom needs to be doing on the wedding day is calling the florist or passing out checks!

If you are determined to go DIY—well go for it! Brides have planned their own wedding for years and years. However, carefully consider your schedule and the amount of time you have to put into planning a wedding. Some weddings are easier to DIY and still, some brides thrive and flourish on the time and detail it takes to plan a wedding. If you choose to be your own wedding planner, prepare yourself by thoroughly researching vendors and pricing in your area. Online forums on wedding websites are full of local information—brides-to-be and the recently wed are more than happy to share their experiences. Even if you DIY your wedding, really consider hiring a wedding planner for the month or two leading up to and for the wedding day . . . you will be thankful that you could enjoy that last dance instead of packing gifts into the car!

SETTING THE DATE

The two most important aspects of planning a wedding are setting the date and location. These two decisions generally need to be made in conjunction with one another, as they are so closely related. You can go about selecting the date and location in the following ways:

- Select a date and then find a location available on that date.
- Select a time frame for your wedding, such as the end of September, the beginning of June, etc. and look for locations that have available dates in that time frame.
- Pick the location you want and accept whatever dates they have available for you to choose from.

You should also consider certain factors that may affect the overall enjoyment of everyone. At first it may seem overwhelming to think about all of these aspects, but considering these factors now, early in the planning, will truly alleviate some stress, burden, and last minute scurrying as the wedding day draws nearer:

- **Typical weather at the time of the year.** Too hot with no shade in August, rainy in November, etc.

- **Local activities and events schedules in nearby areas.** Do you want an airshow taking place at the same time as your outdoor ceremony? It may look really spectacular, but most brides don't envision this!

- **Family events.** You really need to think ahead and not be so wedding-minded when planning. What are your parents going to do if you schedule your wedding for the same day your younger sister graduates from college? That is putting everyone in an awkward place.

- **Travel conditions.** Weddings on long weekends and holidays are great, but you must consider the burden this puts on traveling guests—traffic, long lines, delayed flights, higher ticket prices, etc.

- **Religious holidays and holy days.** Houses of worship may not be available at particular times of the year or it may be in bad taste to plan a celebration on particular days, depending on your beliefs and practices.

LOCATION IS
EVERYTHING!

In today's wedding market, you can exchange vows or hold a reception pretty much anywhere you please, within legal and budgetary considerations, of course. The location you select for your wedding venue speaks volumes about your wedding style and therefore should reflect the tone you envision for the event. From parks to beaches to a private mansion in the hills, you have limitless possibilities.

One of your first decisions to determine a location must be how traditional you wish the wedding to be, including whether or not you will be exchanging vows in a house of worship. If so, the dates available at the house of worship will determine the reception location and even the timing of the festivities. If your parents are involved in the planning or financing of the wedding, it is wise to consult them before deciding whether or not to marry in a religious setting.

Once a ceremony locale is determined you can move onto finding a reception venue. When you select a reception venue you need to look not only at price and capacity issues but also take into account other nuances about the property. The following should be considered when selecting a reception venue:

- Is it handicap accessible?
- Are there enough restrooms, air conditioning, and heating to keep guests comfortable?
- Will it be too hot? Too cold? Too crowded? Too loud?

- What is the distance from the ceremony
  location?
- Does its availability work with the time
  of the ceremony?

The single biggest mistake a bride can make is to fall in love with a location that will essentially use the majority of her budget, leaving little money for other necessities. It would be a shame to have a grand location but not be able to afford a photographer that was capable of handling the job. Be sure to determine a budget before heading out to scout venues and especially before signing any contracts.

DESTINATION WEDDINGS

Destination weddings are an alternative to the "traditional wedding." With families living all over the country and travel becoming a must to attend a wedding anyway, many couples have decided to take the wedding on the road. A destination wedding is essentially getting married anywhere other than where you live (or your family lives). Many couples prefer exotic locales and beaches for a destination wedding, but the mountains, a ranch, or out in a field are all destinations too.

First and foremost when planning a destination wedding you need to research and be very sure of the legal requirements of getting married at that location, especially as it pertains to the legality of the union in the

U.S. Secondly, consider working with a wedding professional, local to your desired destination, to assist you in navigating and perfecting your plans for the event.

There is nothing that dictates the number of guests you can invite to a destination wedding, although typically the numbers of guests at a destination wedding are smaller. However, destination weddings can have 300 guests too. As host of the wedding, the couple is not expected or required to pay for the guests' transportation and lodging expenses, but should cover the costs for all other wedding-related activities.

If you decide a destination wedding is for you, be sure to send a Save-the-Date about eight months in advance (or as soon as possible) so that the guests have adequate time to plan for the trip. Travel and accommodation information should be provided and discounts/rates arranged for the group if possible. Send this information with the Save-the-Date or in a separate mailing as soon as the arrangements are confirmed. Making it easy and enjoyable for the guests is very important.

Chapter 3

The Budget

Planning a wedding is not all fun and flowers and pretty dresses . . . it just looks that way. Behind all the frills and excitement there is the issue of money. For most couples, the budget is a driving force behind how a wedding is planned, what is purchased, and how many guests are invited. Even smart couples have been known to start planning a wedding without really knowing or understanding what is part of the wedding budget, or how it will be paid for.

WHO PAYS

Most people assume the bride's parents will pick up the bill for the majority of the wedding expenses. These expenses are reflected in the outline of traditional responsibilities for the bride's family below. However, creative financing can come into play as you prepare and develop a budget. Before you start deciding who can and should pay, be aware of what the traditional costs are and how they are divided up.

The bride and her family usually pay for:
- Bridal attire
- Invitations
- Ceremony location
- Flowers
- Entertainment
- Groom's wedding ring and gift

- Photography and videography
- Bridesmaids' gifts
- Transportation
- Reception costs

The groom and his family traditionally pay for:

- The engagement and wedding rings for the bride
- The bride's bouquet (although usually it is included with the other floral arrangements) and gift
- Mothers'/grandmothers' corsages and men's flowers (although usually they are included with the other floral arrangements)
- The marriage license
- The officiant's fee or donation in his name

- Housing and gifts for the groomsmen
- The rehearsal dinner

To alleviate some of the financial burden from the bride's family, the groom's parents can assist with some additional financing if they choose and have the means to do so, and the bride's family accepts their offer. In some families such an offer is more than graciously accepted. In other families, the bride's parents may be offended, thinking that this is their duty and responsibility. A frank and open discussion can help resolve most financial issues. Talking money vs. dreams is not romantic and may even be uncomfortable, but keeping the lines of communication open, being realistic, and knowing who is paying for what will help the budget come together.

Some parents expect that when they are handing you a blank check it is an automatic invitation to voice their opinion on wedding matters. Ultimately you and your fiancé should be the ones who get to make these decisions without judgment, but the truth is that sometimes accepting the parent's cash comes at a higher price. Don't let the budget become a power struggle. Be reasonable and include your parents in some of the decisions if they request.

Let's not forget that so many couples marry later in life and have their own jobs, savings, and are totally capable of contributing to the wedding budget. Some couples even finance the wedding themselves, thus eliminating the need to clear any decisions with other family members. Ultimately, there is no reason multiple parties cannot contribute to the wedding budget, and there is no reason anyone who is not directly involved in the nuts and bolts of planning needs to know any of the arrangements.

As the budget is honed and eventually finalized, consider a couple ideas that may steer you in the right direction:

- Hire a wedding planner to assist you with setting up a budget. She is familiar with vendors and what weddings really cost in your area.
- Hold back about 10% of your budget for unforeseen expenses. There are always unforeseen expenses … and if for some reason you are a marvelous budgeter, you will have more money to spend on the honeymoon!

HOW MUCH TO SPEND

There is not a blanket statement that can be made about how much you should spend on your wedding. Celebrity couples spend millions, and it is oh-so-tempting to want to emulate that. But the fact of the matter is that the average wedding for 100-150 guests in the U.S. runs about $28,000. To some brides that is "nothing." To other brides that is a fortune. Investigating the approximate costs of a wedding in your area or the area where you will be getting married will help you establish a budget that fits your life.

The reception venue, including food, beverage, and staffing expenses will amount to the largest piece of the budget. Expect about one-half of your total budget to go towards this portion of the wedding. Try to prioritize the other items of the wedding (photography, flowers, attire, entertainment, etc.) with your fiancé so that you will both be of the same mindset. For example, if photography is important to both of you, but flowers are not, you will know to allot more money for photography and a little less for flowers.

FINANCIAL CONSIDERATIONS

There are so many outside factors that impact the final budget that it is quite difficult to make one single statement about how much a wedding will cost without considering other important factors, such as:

- **Where you live.** The geographic area where you will be holding your wedding will impact the bottom line. The "same"

wedding in a large metropolitan area
will cost more than one in a small town
outside of a major metropolitan area.

- **The date you select.** Prime dates, peak
  season, and holiday weekends may
  incur more expenses due to travel costs,
  which can affect everything from the
  guests' travel to the cost of flowers.
- **Your own personal style/taste.** If you
  grew up in a home where elegant dinner
  parties and grand traditions were the
  norm, chances are a simple reception in
  the church hall may not satisfy your
  dreams.

Many couples forget all about tipping and
gratuities. Check all of your contracts to see
if a gratuity was included; if not, plan on allo-
cating money to tip your vendors. A tip
should be presented as a token of invaluable

service and appreciation. Tipping guidelines vary by geographic location, but
expect to offer higher tips at more upscale
locales and in larger cities.

Chapter 4:

The Ceremony

Today's wedding ceremonies

run the gamut from religious to non-denominational to interfaith to spiritual, meaning your wedding can reflect your personal beliefs, views, and style. Now, we may hear some saying, "I am not a traditional bride. I want my wedding to be my own." Well, rest assured, you can customize a wedding to really say "you." Your wedding will be your own, whether it is traditional or a little out of the box.

TRADITIONAL VS. NON-TRADITIONAL

A traditional wedding includes the elements that many of us are already familiar with—the giving away of the bride, the ring exchange, the kiss. Many assume that a traditional ceremony will take place in a house of worship, and if you are religious or your family has deep roots in a religion, that may be the right path. But you can just as easily have a traditional ceremony in a garden or at home or on the beach. These days, it is about the components of the ceremony more than the location.

The lines between traditional and non-traditional weddings have been blurred. A non-traditional wedding can still have the same formality about it as a traditional wedding. Modern brides borrow traditions and ceremonies from all religions and cultures and even make some up themselves. Determining whether or not you will call your wedding traditional or non-traditional will become quite clear as you begin planning.

If you decide to marry at a house of worship, the rules and beliefs of that location must be adhered to. Some are very strict and others will offer you more leeway in personalizing your ceremony. If a truly non-traditional ceremony is what you desire, consider marrying in a non-traditional location where you have control over all of the aspects of your wedding. Ride a horse down the aisle, have a gospel choir sing as you walk the aisle as husband and wife, or create your own special ceremonies to celebrate the two families becoming one.

When you and if you do decide to step out of the "wedding box," keeping proper etiquette in mind will help keep you on track. You can easily refer to the etiquette outlined for traditional ceremonies and make minor tweaks to have it fit your wedding plan. What is important is to consider everyone's feelings.

WHAT DOES IT INVOLVE?

The ceremony is really what this whole event is all about—proclaiming your love and legally (or spiritually) being joined as a couple. Each state has its own legalities that must be adhered to in order to be joined as a legally married couple in the eyes of the law. Most importantly, for a marriage to be legal, you must obtain a marriage license. The country clerk should be able to provide you with information on marriage licenses and what is required.

Before you begin making plans about your ceremony, you need to know what type of ceremony you would like to have.

- **A religious ceremony** is held in a house of worship, and performed by a religious leader. It is possible to hold a religious ceremony overseen by a religious leader in a non-religious location. (Consult your officiant and house of worship to determine if the marriage will be recognized by the religion before proceeding.)

- **A non-denominational ceremony** has a religious tone but doesn't reflect one particular religion. Non-denominational ceremonies may be held in an appropriate house of worship or other locale.

- **An interfaith ceremony** joins two people from different religions. Whether or not you will be allowed to marry in a particular house of worship will depend entirely on that location's view on interfaith marriage.
- **A commitment ceremony** is held between two people who may not wish to be legally married or by couples who may not be able to be legally married. Many same-sex couples who live in states not recognizing same-sex marriages hold commitment ceremonies.

CONFLICTING RELIGIONS

In today's multicultural world, it is quite common that a couple is combining two different cultures and/or two different religions when they marry. Each couple needs to carefully detail what is important to them when it comes to planning an interfaith ceremony and consider what it means for the future. Many times, the parents will need to be a part of these very serious and sensitive discussions.

As the bride or groom, you do need to be aware that people get very sensitive and even emotional when it comes to religion and maintaining cultural ideals. Handle the situations carefully and with tact to ensure all family members are happy and understanding. Often it is simple misunderstanding of particular traditions and the meanings behind them that lead to strife and conflict.

Of course the issues that may come up with an interfaith marriage reach beyond just explaining it to the family. Some religions will not recognize and some houses of worship will not allow couples of different faiths to marry in their buildings. Still, others will ask for a conversion and/or for extensive studies. Still others may be willing to marry you but not willing to incorporate any "outside" traditions into the ceremony. When two people from very different cultures or religion marry, it is often helpful for the couple to provide wedding programs to the guests that outline the different aspects of the ceremony.

SAME-SEX MARRIAGES

Same-sex marriages have secured a place in the mainstream of our culture, but they do continue to be a source of interest . . . and sometimes controversy. It is impossible to get into the legalities of same-sex marriages or unions, since the laws change continually as more and more states recognize same-sex marriages, but there are some nuances of a same-sex marriage that need to be addressed.

Ultimately this is about two people who love each other celebrating that love and commitment. The basic ideals of etiquette ring true no matter the gender makeup of the couple. When it comes to weddings the same is true for a same-sex couple as it is for a traditional couple—saying "I do" is saying "I do." There is no reason that a same-sex couple cannot enjoy all of the ceremonies, celebrations, and traditions any other couple does on their wedding day.

In a same-sex marriage, there will be times that decisions must be made regarding special ceremonies and other aspects of the wedding. For a traditional couple, it is very clear who are the bride and groom. The bride typically is held in a place of honor—being listed on the invitation first, her parents acting as hosts, wearing the big white dress, etc.

In a same-sex ceremony, the couple can decide if they will both walk the aisle or even decide to walk the aisle together. Couples will also need to make decisions regarding who will be listed first on the invitation, and which set of parents will act as hosts. There may be a preference, or if not, alphabetical order comes into play. Another decision will be how to be introduced at the reception: by their individual names, hyphenated names, or a new married name.

TRADITIONS AND CONSIDERATIONS

Once you know what is traditionally expected in a wedding ceremony, you can
explore the reasons to include or not include
certain traditions. However, before you
begin tweaking to fit your needs, you need to
know what those traditions are. A traditional
ceremony generally includes the following
aspects:

- Processional
- Greeting
- Giving away or presentation of the bride
- Charge to the couple
- Ring exchange
- Pronouncement
- The kiss
- Recessional

Even modern brides are concerned with who will walk them down the aisle. It is no longer as much about being given away, as it is about a show of respect, honor, and love. It is traditional for a bride's father to walk her down the aisle. In Jewish weddings, both parents escort their children down the aisle, and many Christian and non-denominational couples have adopted this tradition. It is a special way to include both mothers and fathers in the ceremony and more and more couples, no matter their religion, are adopting this ritual.

In cases of divorce, the bride's father will still escort her down the aisle, assuming there has continued to be a relationship between the two. If a stepfather has played a significant role, he may be included if you choose, either by having both men walk you down the aisle, or your stepfather escort you halfway and your father the remaining distance, or even both escorting you from the top of the aisle, with the stepfather stopping halfway. If there is tension in the relationship between a bride and her father or the bride's father is deceased, the bride's grandfather, brother, or other special person, even her mother, can escort her down the aisle.

Some see the "giving away of the bride" as antiquated and others see it as an integral part of the wedding tradition. Some women consider this too old-fashioned, and some consider it traditional. Whether you decide to include this tradition is completely up to you. When you reach the end of the aisle with your father, you can skip the actual words altogether and give your father a kiss/hug as you take your place beside your groom, or the officiant can change the wording, asking for "Who blesses this union?"

THE OFFICIANT

You will need to make decisions about where to marry and also who will marry you. When it becomes very complicated due to religious or cultural differences, know that in many areas of the country there are "independent" officiants for hire that represent all religions and spiritual practices. While an officiant for-hire may not appease all the formalities of religious institutions, if you and your fiancé feel it works for you, you may want to look into these options.

The officiant, if a member of a house of worship, does not necessarily charge a fee to perform your wedding, but he generally requests that a donation be made to the house of worship. A thank-you letter and a donation should be presented to the officiant. If the officiant is for-hire, he will generally charge a fee for his services, as he is in essence an independent contractor. Payment is due as per their contract or at the conclusion of the service. The officiant (and spouse) should be invited to the rehearsal dinner and wedding reception.

SEATING SITUATIONS

Seating is important in a traditional ceremony. The ushers seat the guests as they arrive, beginning in the front and filling in pews/chairs. Ushers offer the eldest lady in an arriving party their right arm, with the remaining party following behind. Traditionally the bride's family and friends sit on the left side of the church (facing the altar) and the groom's sit on the right (the opposite is true for Jewish ceremonies). In recent years it has become more and more common for the "sides" to be ignored, but rather, after the immediate family members are seated on the traditional sides, remaining guests are seated as they arrive regardless of "whose guest" they are. If an usher encounters a guest that just won't have this, seat them as they wish.

The first pews/aisles of chairs are reserved for the immediate family of the couple. The parents are seated in the front row. The parents (and sometimes grandparents) are seated just prior to the ceremony beginning as part of the processional. This signifies the ceremony is beginning.

Divorce and remarriage brings up a few questions regarding seating. Most of the time, the relationship between the divorced parties can dictate how close or far away they should sit from one another. The parent who raised the bride or groom is almost always given the seat of honor in the first row (on the respective side). Usually this is the mother, and she is given the opportunity to decide who will sit in the front row with her. The father would sit in the second row, or further back if there is tension. The mother can also decide that the father may sit in the front row as well.

Chapter 5:

The Guests

Once you announce your wedding, there will be many anticipating invitations for the big day. The key to the guest list is balancing it out and keeping within the budget. Creating a preliminary guest list early in the planning stages provides a realistic view on how many people to expect at your wedding . . . and also if you will need to make cuts ASAP.

WHO IS INVITED

Generally, the "must-invite" list includes your immediate family, close family members, your closest friends, the wedding party (and their spouses), and in most cases your boss and his/her spouse. You also should ask your parents and your fiancé's parents who are on their must-invite lists. Unless you are 100% paying for the wedding yourselves, and have no interest in making anyone else happy, you should consult with your parents when devising the guest list.

Distant relatives, long-distance friends, and co-workers are generally on the "I'd like to invite you list," and may or may not make the final cut. Sometimes, couples create "A" and "B" lists for the invitees. They send out invitations to the "A" list and as declines come in, invitations go out to the "B" list. This is a tricky situation. When the "B" invitation is sent too far after the "A" invitations, it becomes very apparent to the "B's" that they are "B's" … and what if plans change for an "A", and they now can come. This can get complicated very quickly. Determine one guest list and stick with it. A little honesty makes for a much smoother process without any backtracking or awkward explaining.

Allowing single guests to bring a date is another frequently asked question. In a world with endless budgets, the answer would be yes. In the real world, you need to make decisions. Long-time established significant others, live-in couples, and domestic partners should be invited. Casual dates are not necessary to invite.

SAVE THE DATE

Save-the-Dates can be a wedding guest's best friend. Rather than having to wait until six to eight weeks before the wedding to schedule travel and other accommodations, guests now can get a head start when couples send out Save-the-Dates. They should be sent up to six months in advance, eight months for a destination wedding. In the Save-the-Date you may include travel information, or make a note that travel information will soon follow.

Save-the-Dates can be formal, casual, or eclectic, but they should reflect the same tone and style you are trying to achieve for your wedding overall. Before Save-the-Dates are sent, a wedding date must be secured, which generally means a venue should be booked, and there should be a tone or theme determined for the wedding. Be sure to not send a Save-the-Date to anyone who is not absolutely 100% on the invite list.

The Save-the-Date should have the following information:
- Bride's full name
- Groom's full name
- Wedding date
- Geographic area of the wedding (you need not include the exact location, but the city and state should be included)
- It can also include a host's name

INVITATIONS

There are so many choices for invitations. Type styles, paper quality, custom made, ordered from a book, sent in a box, recorded on a DVD—you can do just about anything you want. The most important thing to remember is that the invitation style speaks volumes about the tone of your wedding. Order your wedding invitations at least six months in advance to allow ample time for printing and shipping, as well as having the envelopes addressed by hand.

When ordering the invitations know the following:

- **The number of invitations you need (one per couple/family).** It is a good idea to order a few extra at this point. It is much less expensive to order an extra 20-25 now than later.
- **The invitation wording.** Will you include parents' names? The groom's parents' names? A quote?

- **All of the details and the correct addresses and spelling.**
- **Your response deadline and if you need to offer guests a meal choice on the response card.**
- **Is the wedding black tie?** If so, it should be noted.

Wedding invitations consist of the following pieces:

- **The invitation.** It provides the pertinent information and invites the guest to the event.
- **Response card and envelope.** The guests use this card to indicate whether or not they will be attending. It may also ask for a meal choice (if offered). The response envelope should already have a stamp included on it, making it very

easy for the guest to reply.

- **Reception card.** This is used when the ceremony and reception take place in different locations. The card provides the reception information. If the event takes place at one location, print "Reception immediately follows" in the lower left.

- **Map.** Directions or a map on a small card to assist guest(s) with arriving on time to the right location.

- **Inner/outer envelope.** Traditionally the invitation components are stacked and placed in the inner envelope. This is then placed inside an outer envelope. Many are skipping the inner envelope for the sake of cost and being "green."

A traditional invitation (held in a house of worship) is worded as follows:

Mr. and Mrs. Joseph Lee
request the honor of your presence
at the marriage of their daughter
Sarah Marie
to
Mr. Matthew Wood
Saturday, the twenty-second of September
two thousand fourteen
at five o'clock in the afternoon
St. Marks Church
Los Angeles, California

It is proper to use "request the honor of your presence" only on invitations for ceremonies held in a house of worship. For other locales, consider different wording such as "cordially invite" or "request the pleasure of your company."

Addressing wedding invitations always brings up a lot of questions. Here are some basics regarding addressing:

- "And" should only be used to connect the names of two people if they are married.Otherwise, place names alphabetically on separate lines.
- In a case where a couple's names cannot fit on one line, place them on two lines with the second name indented.
- "And guest" or "And family" should be avoided on the invitation, use individual names. Any invited guest over the age of eighteen should receive his/her own formally addressed invitation. (Although most couples include an older child who is still living at home on the same invitation.)
- When you are ready to mail the invita-

tions, take them to the post office and have them weighed. Wedding invitations typically take more postage than other mail.

- A deceased parent should not be listed on the invitation, as a deceased person cannot extend an invitation.

To address envelopes, follow these guidelines:

General addressing (married couple/ couple using the same last name):

Outer envelope:
Mr. and Mrs. John Smith
Inner envelope:
Mr. and Mrs. Smith

NOTE: Some brides want to use the guests' first names on the inner envelope. This is not correct in the world of etiquette, but if your wedding is fairly casual, you can probably get away with it.

When one of the (married) guests has a professional title, the names should be written on one line, with the person with the title listed first:

Outer:
Dr. John Wood and Mrs. Christine Wood
Inner:
Dr. and Mrs. Wood

If both guests are doctors, the envelope should be addressed to:

Outer and Inner:
The Doctors Wood

For couples who are married but use different last names or are unmarried and living together, each person's full name should be on a separate line. The ladies' name is listed first:

Outer:
Ms. Kathy Jones
Mr. Neil Stevens
Inner:
Ms. Jones and Mr. Stevens

When you address an invitation to an entire family, the parents' names are on the outer envelope, and their children's names are added to the inner envelope. The children's names are listed in descending order by age.

Outer:
Mr. and Mrs. John Smith
Inner:
Mr. and Mrs. Smith
Jennifer, Joseph, and Jules

When it comes time to address envelopes of same-sex couples, how you address the envelope will have a lot to do with what you know about the couple, and how they present themselves socially. Are they living together? Are they legally married? Are they spiritually married? What name/names do they prefer to use? If you are unsure of the marital status of a female couple, using the term "Ms." is acceptable, but if you know they are married and/or consider themselves to be married, the term "Mrs." acknowledges their union.

Here are some scenarios and possible addressing solutions.

For a same-sex couple (living together), list the names alphabetically:

Outer:
Ms. Stephanie Andrews
Ms. Kelly Jones
Inner:
Ms. Andrews and Ms. Jones

For a same-sex couple (married and using different last names), list the names alphabetically:

Outer: Ms. Stephanie Andrews

and Ms. Kelly Jones
Inner:
Ms. Andrews and Ms. Jones

For a same-sex couple that consider themselves married either by a commitment ceremony or a legal ceremony (using hyphenated last names):

Outer:
Mrs. and Mrs. Stephanie
and Kelly Andrews-Jones
Inner:
Mrs. and Mrs. Andrews-Jones

For a same-sex couple that consider themselves married either by a commitment ceremony or a legal ceremony (using one last name):

Outer:

Mrs. and Mrs. Stephanie and Kelly Jones

Inner:

Mrs. and Mrs. Jones

After addressing the envelopes, they are ready to be assembled and put in the mail. Stack the invitations from largest to smallest piece. The largest piece is on the bottom and the other pieces in ascending order are stacked on top. Insert the stack of invitation pieces with the wording facing the flap into the inner envelope and then, with names on the inner envelope facing the back of the outer envelope, insert the inner into the outer. Wedding invitations often cost more than a regular piece of mail, so take the entire invitation to the post office to have it weighed.

WHAT ABOUT
THE LITTLE ONES?

Some people love being surrounded by families and children and would not think to have a wedding without them. Some couples have multiple flower girls and ring bearers and invite all of the little ones they know. Others, well, they prefer a quiet, childless event. To indicate that children are not invited, their names would be left off the invitation. For example:

Outer:
Mr. and Mrs. John Smith
Inner:
Mr. and Mrs. Smith

To include the children:

Outer:
Mr. and Mrs. John Smith
Inner:
Mr. and Mrs. Smith
Sarah, Joseph, Marie

There is nothing wrong with having a childless wedding, but couples make the mistake in how those wishes are conveyed. Some couples feel it is okay to include a line saying "An event for adults" or "An adult evening" on their invitation, but this is not in good taste and should be handled through the addressing of the invitations. You can also make sure the parents and wedding party are aware of this desire and have them help spread the word. If you choose to not include children, expect some feathers to be ruffled. Perhaps consider hiring a babysitter and renting a hotel room or room at the facility for the children.

Children in your wedding can be sweet and usually elicit a smile or twenty from the guests. You can have multiple flower girls or ring bearers walk the aisle with you, or you can skip it altogether—it is your prerogative! Do not expect perfection when children are involved, they have minds of their own.

ATTENDEE CONSIDERATIONS

One of the most important things to remember when it comes to guests is that they are just that . . . guests. A guest should not be asked to pay for anything, including

drinks/beverages, parking, restroom attendants, or coat check. As the host, arrangements should also be made for the payment
of services and gratuities for these services.
Additionally, ask the bartender to forgo his
"tip jar." Make your wishes very clear with
the venues and vendors so that guests do
not have to deal with any awkwardness.

When guests make the effort to be a part
of your wedding, it is gracious and customary to say thank you and greet them. Of
course the guests should receive thank-you
notes (see chapter 12) for the gifts they
bring, but they also need to be acknowl-
edged for their presence at the wedding
itself. One way to do this is with a receiving
line. Receiving lines have advantages and
disadvantages. Some are turned off by the
thought of standing in a long line to greet

the bride and groom, but if done correctly this is one way to personally say hello and thank the guest for attending.

The receiving line should include the following people in this order: bride's mother, bride's father, groom's mother, groom's father, bride, groom, Maid of Honor, and bridesmaids. Technically the fathers are not a part of the receiving line, but are generally included. The Best Man does not usually join in the receiving line. The receiving line is formed right after the ceremony, before the reception begins. You need to discuss the proper location for the receiving line. As guests move through the line, greet them, thank them for coming, and most importantly keep the conversation short.

If you forgo a receiving line, the bride and groom need to take time to greet the guests at the event. This does not mean spending twenty minutes with each guest (there is no time for that!), but walking around the room greeting the guests at their tables is acceptable.

The wedding party should also be thanked for the efforts and expenses they have incurred. Warm words of thanks are appreciated, but it is customary to present the members of the wedding party with a gift. The gifts can be personalized for each attendant or you may also present them with matching gifts. Everything from monogrammed money clips for the men to jewelry for the ladies to gift cards to spas or a favorite store or restaurant.

Chapter 6:

Attire

The ring. The flowers. Oh, the fabulous food! But one of the bride's favorite purchases is the gown. There is a lot of emphasis on the attire of not only the bride, but of the bridesmaids and mother of the bride, and as men become more fashion conscious, the groom too! Strictly speaking there are many guidelines to follow regarding the formality of attire vs. the formality of the wedding, but these days, couples make their own rules so selecting attire that reflects the style of the wedding and your personal taste is most important.

THE BRIDE

White is the tradition for a first-time bride's gown. This is still the most popular color choice for brides-to-be. Ivories and blushes have come into favor as has adding accent colors to the traditional gown. Ties, sashes, and bows in subtle and sometimes not-so-subtle colors can add flair to the wedding gown. Rest assured if you choose to go with the traditional white dress, you really cannot go wrong. If you are a second-time bride or an older bride, what is most important is wearing a gown that reflects the formality of the wedding and your age. There are many versions of "white" to choose from.

When you go shopping for the gown, be sure to make an appointment with a salon in advance and have a budget set. One of the first questions a bridal consultant will ask is "What is your budget?" Do yourself a favor and bring along only one to two trusted people (your mom and your Maid of Honor, for example), to avoid having too many opinions, and thus avoid confusion. Before you shop you should also check with the house of worship or your officiant regarding any special rules for dressing. Many religions and cultures have guidelines for appropriate attire.

One prominent accessory for the bride over the years has been the veil and blusher. The blusher is the portion worn over your face and the veil the portion that hangs behind. Neither of these is necessary unless your religion requires your face to be veiled for a portion of the ceremony. Otherwise, it is up to you to decide if this is the appropriate look to complement your gown.

THE BRIDESMAIDS

Bridesmaids come in all shapes and sizes. If you want to dress the ladies in matching gowns, which is typical, it is your responsibility to find a gown that will look nice on all the body types. Another option is to find a designer that offers a line of dresses where you can mix and match sleeves, necklines, etc. There are a few really important things to keep in mind if you are going to dress the bridesmaids in "individual" looks. Keeping the color, fabric, and hemlines consistent will help maintain a unified and stylish look.

Many a bridesmaid has bemoaned the thought of wearing a bridesmaid dress and offered to assist the bride in selecting just the right dress. Well, it is up to you to decide if you want to have any input from the bridesmaids or not . . . if you do, be sure to only ask one or two of them to shop with you.

THE MOTHERS

The mothers of the bride and groom are important players in the wedding look; they will be in many photos and at the center of attention as well. The mothers do not need to wear the same color or style of dress. Their attire should, however, complement one another and the wedding style. For example, one should not be wearing a sexy dress and the other a demure suit. The mother of the bride should shop for her dress first and then communicate her selection with the mother of the groom. Neither of the mothers should wear white, unless the wedding has a white only theme.

THE MEN

Generally the men rent formalwear for the event. If the groom or the fathers own a tuxedo, it may be just fine to wear their own attire. Men can wear rented tuxedos (in the appropriate formality to the wedding) or dark suits. Many men are stretching their fashion muscles and opting for suits in other colors depending on the wedding's theme or tone. The men's attire is accented with a bow tie and vest/cummerbund, a pocket square, or a tie, depending on the groom's style and selection. The fathers often wear the same type of attire as the men in the wedding party. They may distinguish themselves with slightly different accessories or boutonnieres. Ushers who are not groomsmen may wear a dark suit of a rented formalwear.

Chapter 7

The Gifts

A bridal registry is a service that can assist your guests in selecting the perfect wedding gift. While many couples hold off on completing their registries until later in the planning, registering for some items early on in the engagement will provide guests with guidance should they choose to purchase an engagement gift. Many guests expect and rely on bridal registries to help them find a gift the couple needs and appreciates.

WHAT YOU REALLY NEED

Before you hit the stores, you and your fiancé should sit down and go over all of the options, and make some decisions such as which stores to register with. Additionally, think about what color dishes and towels you may want, as well as the style of décor you prefer for your home. Registering at multiple stores is not uncommon in order to cover the wide range of needs a modern couple has or feels necessary.

A bridal registry should be complete with items that you feel are essential to your new home and life together. You should not and do not need to register for any items you do not want or need. For example, some couples feel it is not necessary to register for formal china or silverware or crystal, but think again…this may be the one time in your life that people will buy you such extravagant gifts, and while it may seem impractical at this stage in your life, it may be useful in a few years. On the other hand, if you do not entertain and prefer not to entertain, these items may prove themselves to be useless to you down the line.

REGISTRY ADVICE

Most stores offer a "getting started guide" for registering. You can easily facilitate this process by walking through the rooms in your home and deciding what you feel is needed and important in your life. Every couple has varied needs and there are many stores willing and ready to accommodate your wishes. You are no longer locked into registering for only home goods. You can register for everything from hardware to camping equipment to gardening supplies.

When you register, a store may offer you Bridal Gift Registry cards. These are small cards that often say something similar to "Registered at (insert store name)." Of course they want your guests to shop at their store, but as the bride, you must know it is not proper etiquette to include these cards with your engagement party invitation or wedding invitation. You may, however, include them with the bridal shower invitation, as a bridal shower is specifically for showering the couple with gifts.

That said, you may be wondering how people will find out where you are registered or what to buy you as a gift. Your mother, future mother-in-law, wedding party, and other family members are the key to passing this information along to the guests. It is perfectly acceptable for the registry information to be passed along via word of mouth. Posting that information on your wedding website is also acceptable. Blasting your friends via social media channels would not be considered to be in the best taste.

As you finalize your registry, be sure to register for an adequate amount of items in all price ranges, so that all guests no matter their economic situation can afford to purchase you something you really want or need. You should also diversify your registry to make it easy for your guest to shop the registry. For example, a boutique-style store in one area of the city may not be easily accessible to everyone, so consider also registering at a nationally known store.

Chapter 8:

Vendors and Venues

Essentially you can have your reception almost any place you can afford and legally rent. Couples get married in hot air balloons, on the water, on hilltops, in meadows, as well as at country clubs, ballrooms, and catering halls. Really once you have established your budget the choice is yours. Just be sure to know a little bit about what to expect.

VENUES

On-site venues provide the facility, the catering and staff, and usually the tables, chairs, and other rentals. This type of venue includes everything from hotel ballrooms to banquet halls to restaurants to country clubs. These locales are generally the simplest in terms of planning, as the bulk of necessities are already on site, and usually a location manager is there to help you navigate your way through the particulars as they relate to their venue.

Off-site venues includes beaches, parks, private homes, anywhere that is not already established and set up for a wedding. In locations like this, you are generally renting a location and then it is your responsibility to bring in all the other necessities, including the caterer, tables and chairs, and even trash cans and restrooms. Many full service caterers offer complete planning services to facilitate these types of locations.

There are amazing locations in both categories, it all really depends on the amount of extra time and effort you want to put into the logistical planning of the event. Always be very clear when you sign a contract with the venue, outlining the specific rooms or locations, start and end times, catering arrangements, rental inclusions/exclusions, deposits and payment due dates, cancellations and other policies.

At most sites you will work with a location manager. The job description varies at each location. At some venues the location managers are very hands-on and offer a good amount of guidance, and at other venues the location manager is more hands-off, providing basic information and services. What does this mean? It means that you may or may not get assistance from the location manager when ironing out your details.

Above all, when working with venues and location managers keep your commitments to the venue, pay your bills on time, deliver guest counts on time, and return calls in a timely manner. Good behavior and respect will promote a healthy, friendly work relationship that can only help as you plan.

FOOD AND BEVERAGE

One way or another you will need to serve some food and beverage at your reception. If you have special menu concerns or dietary needs for yourself or your guests, you should look for a caterer that can accommodate those requests. Hence, don't book the finest prime rib restaurant in town and expect them to prepare authentic Chinese food. You will also need to determine if you will serve a sit-down meal or a buffet-style meal.

Consider these other menu particulars:

- When you prepare the menu, you should also be aware of particular cuisines that may offend people. Steer away from serving a menu consisting mainly of unusual items and specialties. That is not to say you cannot serve unique items, but keep the menu non-controversial.

- Include a vegetarian (and maybe even a vegan) option for those guests who do not eat animal products.

- Veganism is a hot topic these days. If you are planning a vegan wedding, be sure to hire a caterer that is vegan and has a track record of catering vegan weddings. A typical caterer may not understand all of the nuances of a vegan lifestyle.

- Other special considerations for catering include kosher offerings. If you have not booked a kosher locale or there is not a kosher kitchen on the property or there are only a few kosher guests, make arrangements to have kosher meals delivered to the venue, giving the hired caterer specific instruction to not touch the kosher meals at all, except for serving.

- You will have at least six to ten different vendors with you on your wedding day that will need to be fed. A handful of them will be with you the entire day. You need to make arrangements to feed your vendors a meal. Most caterers and venues have a special menu and/or a special price so that the vendors may eat as well. It is the best way to keep your vendors happy and on their game. It is also preferable to have a table set up away from the guest's tables—on a balcony, in an adjacent room, etc. for the vendors to eat. No guest wants to eat with the vendors at their table and vice versa.

Brides find all sorts of ways to try and get around paying for the guest beverages. Just stop right there! An invited guest is just that, a guest. A guest should not have to pay for a beverage, including wine or other spirits.

Nowhere does it say you have to serve any alcohol at a wedding. That is your personal decision and your prerogative. You also are not obligated to serve hard alcohol or mixed drinks at your wedding, either. Most couples do tend to serve softer spirits like wine and beer to go along with soft drinks and juices. Work with the caterer to find a beverage plan that works for your budget, but be sure that guests are not paying or tipping the bartender, that is your job.

CAKES

Brides have taken creativity to new heights when it comes to the "wedding cake"; in fact, you really need to call it the "wedding dessert." Cookies, cupcakes, cake pops, pies, dessert in a jar, ice cream sundae bars, fondue bars, dessert stations, crepe station, you name it, a bride (or her wedding planner) has probably thought of it.

No matter what style of "cake" you choose guests are going to expect some sort of cake cutting. They see it as sweet tradition. If the dessert you choose does not lend itself to a "cutting," be creative—share that cupcake, spoon feed each other some ice cream, do something that fits with the style of your wedding that symbolizes a cake cutting, or consider purchasing a small round cake for you and the groom to cut.

If you choose to go the traditional route, it is customary to save that top tier of the wedding cake, freeze it, and enjoy it together on your first anniversary. And, yes, some are appalled when they hear this. But if you wrap that cake really well in layers of plastic wrap, foil, or freezer bags, you can take it out a day or two before the anniversary to thaw and then enjoy it.

A groom's cake is a southern tradition that has grown in popularity. At one time the groom's cake was presented at the reception and then cut and sent home with the guests in boxes. It is still served this way, others cut it and serve it at the reception along side the wedding cake, and still others choose to serve it at the rehearsal dinner. The cake is traditionally chocolate, but if you decide to let him have his cake, you can also let him pick his cake. When it comes to a groom's cake, just about anything goes—team logos, cartoon characters, hobbies, and well, whatever makes him happy.

FLOWERS

Flowers are almost synonymous with a wedding. The bouquets and boutonnieres will be in almost every photo. The flowers at the ceremony frame the event and the flowers at the reception dress the tables. Some brides select flowers for a special meaning, some because they are their favorite, and some because they are in season (and the most cost effective).

The bride's bouquet is distinctive, and "one of a kind." The styles of the other bouquets should complement each other. It would seem odd for the bride to carry a rustic, full bouquet and the bridesmaids something very modern and sleek. The wedding attendants are presented with flowers, usually bouquets, to carry during the wedding.

The Maid of Honor sometimes receives a slightly different bouquet to distinguish her from the bridesmaids.

The groom and groomsmen also traditionally receive a boutonniere. There have been boutonnieres that are very overwhelming, and quite frankly most men are not overly concerned with them. When you talk to your florist make it very clear what size you want your boutonnieres to be. A modern version of the boutonniere is to have the groomsmen sport coordinating pocket squares.

The parents and even grandparents typically receive flowers to distinguish them from the guests. The ladies often receive a corsage, but be careful in your selection; heavy corsages can damage the ladies delicate dresses. Consider a wrist corsage or a small bouquet for them or go ahead and ask their preference. The men can wear a boutonniere or whatever the groomsmen have decided to wear.

When selecting the flowers you should take into account the fact that many guests may have allergies, and that the scent of some flowers may overpower the room and even compete with the flavors of the food. Be especially sure to ask the wedding party and families if they have any allergies to avoid an attack at the altar. Also talk to the florist about managing the scents of the floral displays.

ENTERTAINMENT

There is a long standing debate about bands vs. disc jockeys. Some view it as a matter of "taste" but preference and budget also plays a big part in the selection. DJ's are not inexpensive but generally cost less than a band. A DJ can play just about any song you wish, as you know it. A band provides live powerful sounds, but will be performing cover versions of the songs you know and love. Most guests consider bands to be more upscale and high end. Due to manpower alone, bands are more expensive than a DJ. A lot of couples combine live music with recorded music, incorporating live musicians into the ceremony and cocktail hour and a DJ for the reception.

As you make your selections, remember a few things. Be sure the musicians are professional and will come dressed appropriately. Be sure they are experienced at handling weddings. In the case of bands, playing at a wedding is much different than jamming at the local bar. The bandleader or DJ will act as your emcee for the evening, so he should be comfortable, smooth, and have a good voice. Be sure to offer the entertainment a meal, but be clear that they are not to partake in any alcoholic beverages.

PHOTOGRAPHY AND VIDEOGRAPHY

The photographer and videographer are hired to capture the magical moments and memories of the day. They will be the vendors, other than a wedding planner, that spends the most time with you. Choose wisely. If he/she is driving you crazy at the first interview, do you really think it will be less annoying on your wedding day? Be careful to hire a photographer and videographer that you can work with personally and professionally. Also, ask the photographer about providing an engagement photo session prior to the wedding so you all can work together and get familiar with one another.

Many couples prefer photographers and videographers that are less obtrusive and capture the moments as they unfold, rather than dictating and forcing situations. A professional photographer or videographer will know how to capture these special unscripted moments as well as throw in the more formal posed shots that you know your mom wants! If you have ideas regarding certain poses or shots you want to have captured, talk to the photographer about them and create a shot list, but be careful not to dictate too much or be too specific so as to not lose any spontaneity in the day.

Many photographers encourage the bride and groom to take photos prior to the ceremony. However, tradition dictates the bride and groom do not see each other until you walk down the aisle (in the Jewish tradition, the couple does sometimes see each other prior to perform Jewish ceremonies). Taking the photos before the ceremony serves many purposes: it speeds up the photo taking process, leaving the couple more time to enjoy their guests after the ceremony, the couple looks fresh—no tears (yet), and no lipstick on the cheeks. It is ultimately your decision, so be sure not to be pushed into doing what you do not want to do.

If you choose to see the groom prior to the ceremony, work with the photographer and videographer to make that moment memorable. You can request they stay back for the first meeting or you can have them right there capturing that first sighting. It works best when the bride and groom (along with the photographer and videographer) are taken some place private for this meeting, making it special and memorable for the two of them.

Having your hair and makeup professionally done will also contribute to the appeal of your wedding photos. Professional hair and makeup stylists know how to make that hair stay put for a day and use the best product to ensure you're still picture perfect after the ceremony and through the reception. Professionals will often travel to your location to get you ready, alleviating the stress of travel.

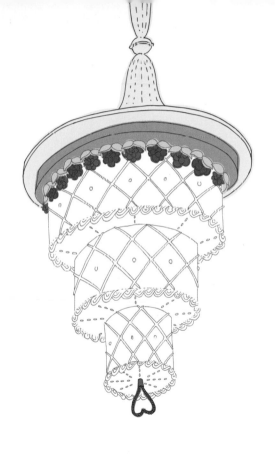

Chapter 9

The Parties

The wedding reception is a big party, probably the biggest party you will ever plan and host . . . but guess what? As bride and/or groom, you actually get to attend and be honored at parties you do not have to plan or pay for. Celebrating with your friends and families is one of the most joyous aspects of a wedding celebration. Enjoy this time of your life and enjoy the parties.

THE BRIDAL SHOWER

The purpose of the bridal shower is the opportunity to be presented with gifts and necessities to outfit your home and prepare you for married life, while sharing some special time with the ladies in your life. The shower is held anywhere from a few months up to a few weeks prior to the wedding, depending on scheduling and the locale of the event. A few months is preferable, but sometimes it is easier to host a shower within a few days of the wedding date if the majority of the guests are from out of town, rather than asking them to make major travel plans twice.

The bridal shower may be held in a restaurant, event venue, or someone's home, and is typically hosted by the Maid of Honor in conjunction with the bridesmaids. The bride's mother or immediate family (sisters) should not host the event, as it is seen as impolite and as though the family is asking for gifts. That said, often a bride's sister is her Maid of Honor or in the wedding party, so this may be acceptable. Sometimes the groom's friends/family also want to throw a shower, and this is just fine, but the same rules apply in regards to the immediate family hosting as they did with the bride's family. It is perfectly acceptable for a bride to have more than one bridal shower.

Only ladies who are invited to the wedding should be invited to a bridal shower, but that does not mean that every woman invited to the wedding needs to be invited to the shower. If you are having multiple showers, be sure to not "over-invite" the ladies.

Guests need not be invited to more than one shower. In the case of the bridesmaids, they may be invited to multiple showers, but make it clear that they are not expected to continually purchase gifts. One major etiquette faux pas to avoid—inviting guests to a gift giving event that celebrates a wedding when they will not be a part of it.

Since the purpose of a bridal shower is to bestow the bride with gifts, it is perfectly acceptable to talk about registry information and include it with the invitation. There is usually food served and a cake or special dessert. Many times the ladies play wedding or marriage-related games, and then it all culminates with the bride opening her gifts.

THE BACHELOR/
BACHELORETTE PARTIES

Just the term bachelor/bachelorette party causes angst for some. These parties have a reputation for involving a lot of alcohol, a lot of partying, and a lot of potential trouble. But they do not have to live up to these low expectations. Among other ideas, sporting events and spa days are viable alternatives that can get you in a lot less trouble.

The honor attendants are the main organizers of this party and can absolutely ask the other attendees to contribute to paying for the bride's way. Invitations can be printed and mailed, passed along by word of mouth, or a phone call. An email is an acceptable invitation depending on the formality of the overall wedding experience.

These parties are held prior to the wedding, anywhere from a couple months to a couple days, although holding one too close to the wedding is discouraged, unless unavoidable due to traveling schedules and details. These parties are smaller in size than a bridal shower, and usually include the bride's or groom's closest friends who want to go out and celebrate "the end of your single days."

THE REHEARSAL DINNER (OR LUNCH)

The rehearsal dinner or lunch is held in the days just prior to the wedding, usually the night before, immediately following the ceremony rehearsal. This event is traditionally hosted by the groom's family, leaving his parents in charge of the invitations, menu, and all points in between for this night. Hopefully his parents will consult with you, both in regards to invitees, menu, formality, and locations. Be sure to approach them before they begin their planning to work out any special requests.

The guests include: the bride's parents, groom's parents, the officiant and his/her spouse/significant other, siblings, grandparents, and the wedding party and their families, and anyone else (readers, soloists, greeters) who was at the rehearsal. That is already a pretty large guest list, but the bride and groom can invite other close friends or relatives or out of town guests if budget and space permit. It is important to be consistent when inviting those to the rehearsal dinner so as to not hurt feelings. For example, will Aunt Mary be upset if Aunt Jane is invited and not her? Probably.

The rehearsal dinner can be casual or it can be more formal. There are no rules to dictate this; the one factor you need to keep in mind is that it should not eclipse the style of the wedding itself. For example, if you are having a simple mid-afternoon affair in the garden, a five-course sit down dinner at the finest restaurant in town may be a little over the top. The rehearsal dinner is everyone's chance to be relaxed, toast one another, and share stories in a more intimate environment. The bride and groom also may present the attendant's gifts, as well as gifts (if any) to their parents.

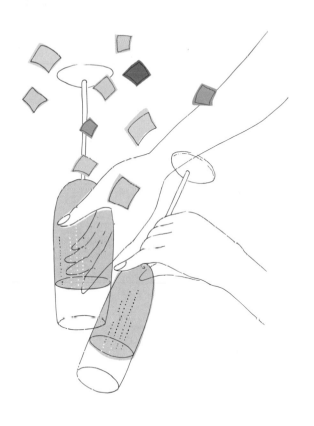

Chapter 10

The Reception

The reception is the time to celebrate with family and friends, and probably the biggest party you will ever host. The tone and style of the reception should be carried over from the ceremony and other wedding activities for the events to flow nicely together. The reception should be scheduled to begin within a reasonable amount of time after the ceremony ends. Large gaps of time between the ceremony and reception make for bored and sometimes hungry and angry guests.

You can make your wedding reception be

just about anything you want. Gorgeous photos in magazines of over-the-top receptions are pretty to look at, but not the reality for most couples. A reception does not have to be extravagant or deplete your bank account. It can be simply elegant beverages and hors d'oeuvres or it can be a five-course dinner, as long as the menu and formality is appropriate to the time of day.

SEATING DISCUSSIONS

So many couples ask the question, "Why do we need a seating plan?" The answer is because it makes guests feel like they have a place to sit, a place to be, which then makes them feel more comfortable and creates an overall atmosphere of ease at the reception. No one ever said devising the plan was easy, but it is truly appreciated by the guests.

When creating the seating plan, group guests into categories: family with family, college roommates with college roommates, work associates with work associates. Generally you will know if there is tension amongst any guests and seat them as far away from one another as possible. Don't try to play matchmaker at the wedding, even if you are tempted. Keep the single guests happy and comfortable by seating them with their other family and friends.

Keeping the bride and groom front and center is one of the most important aspects of seating at a reception. It is all about you! There are multiple variations on seating that couples come up with to suit their particular needs, but here are a few of the most popular seating options:

- **A sweetheart table** is a smaller table just for the couple. In this instance, the members of the wedding party may be seated all together at tables near the couple, or the dates/spouses of the wedding party may sit with them at the tables. The parents' tables would also be near the wedding party and couple.

- **The head table** includes not only the couple but the members of the wedding party as well. Traditionally the wedding party would alternate between bridesmaid/groomsmen at the table with the Best Man sitting next to the bride and the Maid of Honor next to the groom. Small children who are members of the wedding party should sit with their parents.

- **A couple can sit with their parents**
  at a table near the front and center of the
  room. If the bride's or groom's parents are
  divorced, use the same logic as the ceremony, sit with the parent who raised you
  and the other parent (and spouse) can sit
  nearby, if they cannot all sit at one table.

The parents and grandparents are also
seated in places of honor at the reception,
usually at tables near the front of the room
very close to the bride and groom. The officiant and his companion should also be
invited to the reception and if they choose to
attend should be seated with the bride's
family. If there is tension in the family, do
your best to separate these people by plac-
ing them on opposite sides of the room.

The venue should supply you with a floor plan for developing the seating chart. Once you have the tables and guests matched up, an alphabetized master seating list needs to be made, as do escort cards. Escort cards have the guests' names and table number printed on them and are picked up at the entrance to the reception. The escort cards direct guests to their table. Once the guests arrive at the table, they may either take any available seat, or if the couple has chosen, look for their place card, which designates a particular setting at the table.

TRADITIONS TO FOLLOW (OR IGNORE)

Wedding receptions are rich with tradition and ceremony. Some of those traditions are sweet and meaningful and others need to just slip quietly away. Before you plan out the events of your reception, take a look at these traditions and decide which ones you are keeping and which ones you are tossing! Get familiar with the traditions below:

- **The Grand Entrance** occurs at the reception and is the formal introduction of the bride and groom. The couple is announced by their married names and this signifies the party is ready to begin. Sometimes the entire wedding party and/or parents are included in the entrance.

- **The first toast** of the evening is proposed by the Best Man. This toast is generally made early in the event, leaving plenty of time for others who wish to make toasts as the event progresses.

The Maid of Honor may offer a toast as well. Toasting does not have to be done with champagne or sparkling wine. It may be done with whatever the guests are drinking. When the toasts are proposed, the couple needs to remember this is a toast for them. Be attentive, look gorgeous, and when everyone else takes a sip at the end of the toast, you should refrain, as you should not drink to yourself. If the emcee signals the guests to stand, the couple should remain seated. If everyone is already standing, the couple may remain standing.

- **Many times the father of the bride has paid for the wedding or a portion of the wedding and finds it polite to welcome the guests.** This welcome is very much like a toast to the couple and to thank the guests for coming.

- **Some couples choose to have the officiant bless the meal.** This would depend on the religious tone of the wedding in general.

- **The first dance** of the reception is danced by the bride and groom. Once the couple has taken their first turn on the dance floor, the dance floor is considered to be open to all guests. Generally the first dance takes place earlier in the course of the events for this reason. Many couples enjoy performing their first dance right after the Grand Entrance, as all eyes are already on them. If not the dance may take place between courses or right after the meal service is finished. The dance can be choreographed to a "T" or a simple and sweet dance.

- **During the father/daughter dance** the bride and her father share a sentimental moment on the dance floor. Many times the groom and his mother will join in as well, or dance to their own song. In the case of divorce, the bride may dance with the father who raised her (usually who walked her down the aisle), share a dance with a father and stepfather (or have two dances), or dance with another special man such as a grandfather or brother or uncle. If the bride's father is deceased or not present, the bride may dance with another significant male in her life or skip this dance altogether.
- **The cake cutting** is done about one hour after the meal has been finished. This is also a great time for the couple to make a toast to one another or thank the

guests for coming. The bride and groom cut the cake together with the bride's right hand on the knife and the groom's hand atop hers, although many photographers will ask you to reverse it so that they can see the ring! Using the cake service the couple should cut a small piece of the cake and place it on a plate, and then gently feed each other a small bite with a fork. Somewhere along the way, couples found it fun to smash the cake into one another's face. Many couples continue to do this or are afraid their spouse will. Truly this is one portion of the tradition that needs to be retired. No bride or groom looks good with cake up their nose.

- **The garter toss** is a tradition that is currently out of favor with many modern couples. In essence the bride sits on a chair and the groom reaches under her gown to find the garter and then tosses it into a crowd of single male guests. The lucky one to catch the garter is supposedly the next male to marry.

Raunchy emcees and overzealous grooms have taken this tradition to the extreme and really tarnished the ritual.

Also depending on your age and who is at your wedding, you may want to reconsider participating in this—your boss may not need to be a part of this display! But by all means if you want to do this, just do it with tact and class, and perhaps a touch of subtlety.

- **The bouquet toss** is the bride's version of the garter toss. All of the single ladies gather in an open area (usually the dance floor) and the bride, with her back turned, tosses the bouquet into the crowd of ladies, with legend saying the lady who catches it will be the next to marry. Seems sweet, no? Well, those ladies can go crazy for that bouquet. On the other hand some single female guests feel a bit embarrassed being singled out as the single girl at the wedding.

A bride generally knows her crowd and can make a decision whether or not to do this. An alternative to the bouquet toss is to have the bride honor someone special—her mother, grandmother, special relative, or even the mother of the groom—by presenting the bouquet to her.

- **The exit** is simply that, the formal and official way the couple leaves the reception. This exit can be full of pomp and circumstance with sparklers, bubbles, or rose petals being thrown as the couple exit to a grand limousine or car to whisk them away. Or the couple can simply dance a last dance and walk quietly out of the venue together.

GIFTS

When the wedding is over, there will be gifts to attend to. The gifts need to be loaded in a specific car or taken up to a hotel room for safekeeping. Moving the gifts is not something the bride and groom need to be doing on their wedding night. Ask a trusted family member or friend, along with the wedding planner (if you have one) to be in charge of the gifts, ensuring they arrive at the proper destination. Always ask someone to move cash and gift cards to a safe place early in the event. Ask someone in charge of the gifts if they will also be responsible for delivering the cake top wrapped to the freezer at your home (if you are carrying out this tradition)

Gifts are not opened at the reception. In certain areas of the country it is a tradition and very much expected that the bride's parents host a gift opening. This is a smaller, less formal event held at the parent's home the day following the wedding. At this time, the couple opens their gifts, and guests may come and watch. In other areas of the country, this is purely a personal preference rather than an expectation. Not sure what to do? If you have been invited to many gift openings then it is probably tradition in your area, expect to plan a gift opening.

Chapter 11:

The Honeymoon

You worked hard for this most coveted and highly anticipated vacation, perhaps the vacation to end all vacations… the honeymoon! The honeymoon is an important consideration when settling into life as a married couple. For months and months, you and your fiancé plan this amazing event to celebrate your love, but in that planning you sometimes lose sight of being a couple. The honeymoon is the perfect antidote for that!

PLANNING THE TRIP

Planning and paying for the honeymoon is one of the groom's biggest responsibilities. The bride will probably be very involved with selecting a locale and the type of honeymoon, as many couples share the planning on most of the wedding details. Just like coveted wedding venues, coveted honeymoon locales get booked in advance. With so many weddings taking place during peak travel seasons, resorts and hotels may sell out, but not if you prepare and start planning that honeymoon right away.

One really important aspect of traveling for the honeymoon is that the bride's travel is booked in her maiden name (or whatever name is on her driver's license or passport). Of course you can check into the hotel as

Mr. and Mrs., but you will not yet have new identification that reflects your married name, and if you do not book the travel correctly, you may not be allowed to board a plane or ship, thus never making it to the final destination!

Arrangements should be made for a housesitter while you are away. You have a home full of gifts and chances are good that more gifts may arrive on your doorstep in the days and weeks following the wedding. It would be a pity to have missing or ruined gifts. Also be sure to make arrangements for any pets in advance!

PREPARING FOR THE TRIP

You will need to pack well for a honeymoon—everything from sunscreen to medications to the perfect outfit! Some destinations require more preparation and research. Investigate travel websites and local guides for tips and tricks when traveling to the area. Look into weather patterns, local customs, and attractions. Do your homework prior to your trip to ensure a great experience.

Do you have to spend every minute together on your honeymoon? Well, no, you do not. There just may be the possibility that he wants to go rock climbing and you want a massage at the spa. While the purpose of a honeymoon is to be together, spending some time to do what makes you happy and refreshes you is also important.

Just as expressing gratitude to your service providers was important on the wedding day, it is important on the honeymoon, too. Don't be caught off guard. Tipping is common and expected at most resorts, on cruise ships, and at many finer hotels (or course there are some all-inclusive resorts that handle this differently). Be sure to bring cash (local to your destination) in small bills: $1's, $5's and a few $10's for easy tipping.

Chapter 12:

Post-Wedding To-Do's

You planned a wedding. You got married. You went on a honeymoon . . . and now you are back home and back to reality. While you may still be basking in the bridal glow it is time to get down to business and tie up the loose ends. You may enjoy looking at the gorgeous stacks of wedding gifts; in fact you may already be using some of them. And you may have verbally thanked the giver, but nothing can replace a thoughtful, well-written thank-you note. Yes, no texts, no emails, no social media posts can replace the traditional thank-you note.

THANK-YOU NOTES

Upon returning from your honeymoon, thank-you notes should be the first order of business. You will simply need some note cards and envelopes, addresses (which you should already have), a good pen, stamps, and then it is time to get to work. Thank-you notes should be handwritten, not computer generated, and mention the following: a greeting/opening, a mention of the gift, a mention of how you plan to use the gift, a special thought or memory to close, and be signed by you or your groom (whoever wrote the note). In the case of monetary gifts, you should not mention the dollar amount, but you should mention the gift, calling it a "thoughtful gift" or something similar and also mention how you plan to use the gift.

But what if the gift is awful? If a gift you received was something that is not your taste, not your style, and not on your registry leaving no recourse for where to return it? Well, it is not worth offending the giver by asking where he got it so you can take it back. Sometimes you just need to put a smile on, write a sweet thank you, and keep it.

Somewhere out there is a myth that you have one year to write thank-you notes. This is not the case. Thank-you notes should be written as soon as possible, but within a few months of the wedding date. Hopefully you have already written all of those thank-you notes from the engagement party and bridal showers.

NAME CHANGES

Once upon a time, women changed their names to their new spouse's name. That is no longer always the case and there is no right or wrong answer across the board. Ultimately, you decide what is best for you. Some options for the name game include:

- Taking your spouse's/husband's name.
- Keeping your maiden name.
- Adopting your maiden name as your middle name and your spouse's/husband's name as your last name.
- Hyphenating your maiden name and spouse's/husband's last name.

When you go to change your name, be consistent across the board. You will need to change:

- Social security card
- Driver's License
- Passport
- Savings and retirement accounts
- Bills/credit cards/utilities
- Association memberships/directories

Your first step to change your name is to apply for a new social security card, then the driver's license and passport, and so on. While the task may seem daunting, doing all of these important documents at once may save you time in the end.

THE DRESS

Once the wedding is over, the bride is left with one very large, very expensive souvenir … her wedding dress. Saving your wedding dress is a tradition. Many brides save their dresses in the hopes that one day their daughter would wear it (just realize she may not want to!) or simply for sentimental reasons. The choice is completely personal and totally yours.

If you do save the dress, having it professionally cleaned and packaged is important to preserve its beauty and the delicate fabric and adornments. If you choose not to save your dress, you can resell the dress in a local shop or salon or even on eBay, just do not expect to get full market value. A wedding dress is a little like a car—once you drive it off the lot, the value decreases. Another option is to donate the dress to a charity, which will then resell the dress with the profits going to benefit that charity. You do not need to make these decisions right away.

You may need to sit on the decision for a bit and really consider your options, but you should have the dress cleaned soon, especially if there are major stains on it.

FINAL TO-DO

Enjoy your new life as a married couple!

Notes

Notes

Notes